D0434229

EVEN MORE CLASSROOM CLANGERS

Best Wishes

[signature]

Even MORE CLASSROOM CLANGERS

Author · JOHN G. MUIR   Illustrations by GEORGE J. GLASS

MAINSTREAM
PUBLISHING

For Mum

Copyright this selection © John G. Muir 1989
© Illustrations George J. Glass
All rights reserved

First published in Great Britain 1989 by
MAINSTREAM PUBLISHING COMPANY (EDINBURGH) LTD
7 Albany Street
Edinburgh EH1 3UG

Reprinted 1989

No part of this book may be reproduced or transmitted in any form or by any other means without the permission in writing from the publisher, except by a reviewer who wishes to quote brief passages in connection with a review written for insertion in a magazine, newspaper or broadcast.

British Library Cataloguing in Publication Data
Even more classroom clangers.
 1. Humour in English, 1945 — Special Subjects:
Education — Anthologies
I. Muir, John G.
827'.914'080355

ISBN 1–85158–263–0

Typeset in 11/13pt Bembo by S B Datagraphics, Colchester
(An Ician Group Company)

Printed in Great Britain by Richard Clay Ltd, Bungay, Suffolk.

Acknowledgements

This book follows in the tradition of *Classroom Clangers* and *More Classroom Clangers*, thanks to the many people who have sent me their own favourites. Young people have passed on recent experiences and many retired teachers have written me cheery letters with stories they recall from their own time in schools. As with my previous two collections I am aware that many may be apocryphal but for most of us they are sure to be fresh in the telling.

If I tried to list the names of everyone who has contacted me I would be certain to leave someone out but I have to mention Fiona Smith and Robert Boote who were kind enough to allow me to dip into their own lengthy jottings from pupils they have met.

It has also been a pleasure to work again with my illustrator George J. Glass, who has patiently responded to changes I have requested and has slaved night and day to meet deadlines for publication.

John G. Muir,
Dornoch,
Sutherland.

CONTENTS

Telling Tales

Having reprimanded a boy for showing off pages from a girlie magazine, which the pupil said he had found in the school waste-paper bin, the headmaster thought he had better make an announcement. *"Now, if anyone finds anything like that again, you must show it to me first."*

Every morning at 8.30 he could be seen waking up to school.

A parent was intrigued when her little daughter said that the teacher was wearing a wig all week. *"How do you know that it's a wig?"* she asked.
"Of course it is, I see her putting it on every day."
The situation was clarified when the mother saw her walking down the road from school one day wearing a fur hat!

A pupil in a class made a rude remark under his breath but would not own up. The teacher threatened to punish the whole class if the person did not stand up immediately. He spoke to each one in turn but nobody confessed so he began to punish everyone. When he came to the last one he was both exhausted and exasperated and said, *"Now if you tell me who did it I'll let you off but if you don't you will get more than anyone else."*
"Okay, Sir," came the quick response, *"I did it."*

Ann, a red-haired "hard nut" in an upper secondary school arrived in class having obviously been recently involved in a fight. The teacher, "concerned" for her welfare, enquired as to the reasons for the fracas and learned that she had been involved in a fight with another girl. Ann admitted that she had started the fight but was reluctant to tell why. After some persuasion she confessed, in a broad Scottish accent, *"She called me a bad name, Sur. I cannae tell ye whit it wis, but it starts wi' an H."*

In another incident the same Ann was stopped in the corridor, apparently skipping a class. When asked where she thought she was going, she replied casually, *"A'm suppost tae be at Sex wi' Mr Sutherland but ah cannae find him."*

Anybody who speaks French could teach it to a class of 14-year-olds.

The difference between *external* and *internal* fertilisation is that some animals mate inside and some do it in the open air.

At this stage in its life cycle, the butterfly is called a grub because it is always eating.

As a gentle introduction to sex education, a teacher decided to talk about the life cycle of the frog. They visited a local pond and one of the children noticed a male frog on the back of a female frog. The pupils were curious to know what was happening so the teacher explained. On hearing this, one little girl, in a rather loud whisper, exclaimed, *"I'll tell you one thing. There's no way my mummy would let my daddy jump on her back like that!"*

The difficulty which children have in appreciating adult imagery is highlighted in the following humorous but sobering account of one child's misunderstanding of advertising about AIDS.

The class was discussing Cold Lands and icebergs were mentioned. One boy said, *"Sir, you can catch AIDS from icebergs, can't you?"*

Realising that the boy was quite serious, the teacher asked him why he thought that and learned that the fellow had seen a warning leaflet with the caption, *"AIDS, it's only the tip of the iceberg."*

An eight-year-old came home from school one day and announced to his mum that they had learned all about where babies come from. Interested to know how much he had been told, she asked him to tell her all about it.

He was just finishing the rather long and detailed account, when his father arrived home. *"Tell dad all about it too Roger,"* said mum.

With an exasperated look, he exclaimed, *"Why? Does he not know either?"*

Two pupils arrived late for school. The first one, faking a sore hand, said that he had been stung by a bee. *"And what's your excuse?"* the teacher asked the other boy.

"Please, Sir, the bee stung me too," **he replied, holding his hand also.**

"But a bee only stings once," **said the teacher, grinning.**

"In that case it must have been a wasp, Sir," **they added, in unison, smiling.**

If you are looking for the janitor, he can be found dealing with a problem in the girls' toilets.

It is now too late to send for the *Early Starters in Maths* sample pack.

Staff should note that suspension from classes is not an appropriate punishment for truancy.

The infant staff are collecting toilet rolls. Please pass on used ones to them.

Any pupil wishing to take part in throwing the discus can practise with Mr Smith any afternoon this week.

Nursery School Circular: Please return any underwear borrowed from the headteacher as she may need it in case of "emergencies".

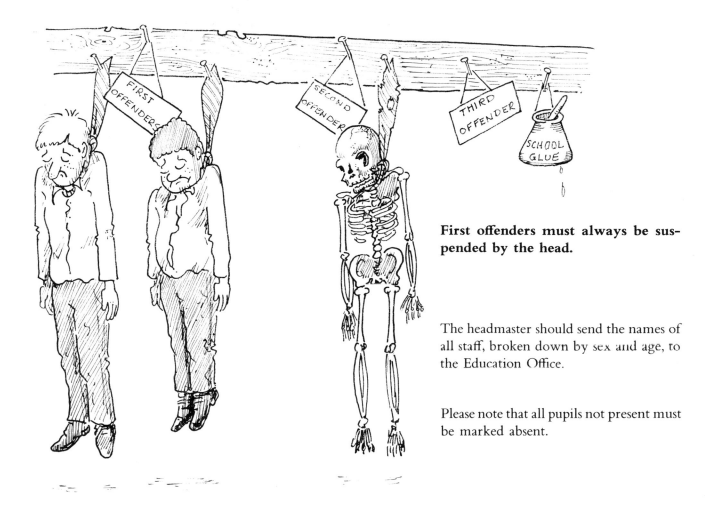

First offenders must always be sus-pended by the head.

The headmaster should send the names of all staff, broken down by sex and age, to the Education Office.

Please note that all pupils not present must be marked absent.

Pay differentials should be increased.

Dear Teacher

I must inform you that Julie McFarlane lost her peace, she says it was stollen. I am telling you because I do not want it to become a habbit.

Peter stayed off because of bad pans in his head. We have always known that this was his week part.

I am sending this note because John will be late on account of his having to take his father's breakfast.

My husband and I feel that William should drop history as we both feel there is no future in it.

Susan did not come back to school after lunch because her dad turned into a big tree on his way home from work.

Bad punctuation, not a knighthood, gives us this letter: Sir John stayed off because he cut his arm badly in a fight.

Patricia had to take the day off as we were flitting and had to take her with us.

When we took her to the doctor because of the palpitations we kept her at home. I have to tell you, however, that her heart is still beating.

When Lorna came home she had bad pains in her stomach so we kept her at home to see what would come out of it.

There is really no point in him doing French because if he follows in his father's footsteps he will never leave the farm.

Latin is a dead language anyway and as far as my son is concerned the longer it stays that way the better.

Please excuse David for being off last week. He had diarrea for three days and it took him the other three days to get over it.

Peter was absent from school yesterday as he had entered the world record of "how many times can one be sick over a twenty-four hour period."

. . . I am yours trully, his father.
P.S. It wasn't my fault.

Robert has been accused of stealing and that may well be the case but I am prepared to take his word for it as it is a long while since he has taken anything.

Your letter asking me to a meeting about the new school boards surprised me because I didn't think that blackboards should be the concern of the PTA.

Robert came home today and told us that a teacher had said that he was illiterate. I have to tell you that this is not the case as we were married five years before we had him and have his birth certificate to prove it.

Please excuse Billy. It's his head. It's being coming off and on all weak.

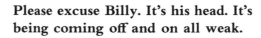

We kept her off school because she came out in a rush.

I was very surprised to get your letter on how to deal with head lice. I thought this sort of thing was a thing of the passed.

More money is being spent on education than ever before.

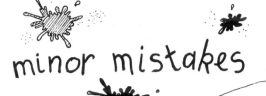

minor mistakes

Two older pupils came into the school during the interval half carrying an infant, who was rubbing his leg as if in great pain. *"It was a big black labrador, Miss,"* said the little lad. *"Did it bite you?"* asked the concerned teacher.

"No, Miss, it just tasted me," whimpered the infant.

Talking about what they might do when they grew up, one little lad thought that being a fireman or an engine driver would be a bit boring. *"I want to be a teacher,"* he shouted out, *"so that I can boss people about."*

A little boy was given a row at the breakfast table by his mother. He ran upstairs, crying and shouting that he wasn't going to school and hid under the bed. When his dad appeared at the table he asked what the row was about and then went upstairs to have a word with his son. To humour the lad a little he crawled under the bed beside him. Before he could say anything, the boy, drying his tears, chipped in with, *"Has she given YOU a row too dad?"*

A couple of little girls were boasting about how much they were allowed to do around the house to "help" their mum. One said that she laid the table every night for dinner and helped peel potatoes. *"That's nothing,"* piped up the other, *"I'm allowed to make my own toast AND I'm allowed to scrape it myself."*

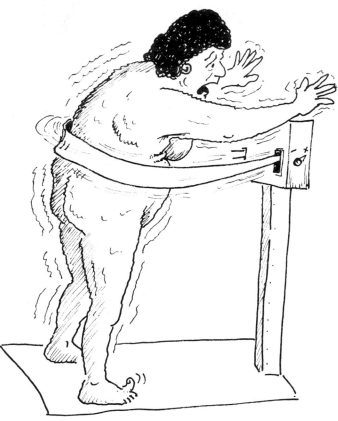

My daddy has bought a waist disposal unit for my mum.

After what the teacher considered to be a very interesting lesson, she was more than a little dismayed when none of the children wished to comment or ask any questions. *"Have you no questions at all you want to ask?"* she said.
"Please Miss, can we ask any question?"
"Certainly Susan, anything."
There was a pause and a giggle and then, *"Please Miss, do you know that you've got a big black hair on your chin?"*

The little girl was being given a writing lesson, the teacher holding her hand and guiding it across the page. *"Now you try it, Jenny,"* she said, letting go of her hand. *"But the pencil won't go, Miss,"* she replied with a puzzled look on her face.

Mothers are often more upset than their offspring when they have to leave them at school on the first day. Clearly this was the case with one parent, when a little girl played with her friends while her mother hovered around anxiously in the background. After a while, the girl said, *"Don't worry, Mum, you can go home now, I'll come and see you at lunchtime."*

Having been told that a noun was a person, place or thing a pupil gave as an example "an organist". Thinking it to be an unusual reply, the teacher asked why he had chosen that word. *"Because that's a person that plays a thing, isn't it?"*

When a four-year-old, who was the youngest of four boys, returned home from his first day at school, his mother asked him, "*Well, did you have a nice time today?*"

"*Yes, I did,*" he replied.

"*And did you make some friends?*"

"*Yes,*" he said.

"*And what were they called?*"

After thinking for a minute, the little fellow replied, "*I think they were called **girls**.*"

The infant mistress decided to move round the groups of newly enrolled pupils just as the last of the mothers were leaving the classroom. Seeing one little girl looking a bit sad, she sat down in an empty chair beside her. Before she could offer any words of encouragement, the lass piped up, "*Has your mummy just gone too?*"

When the five-year-old was asked why he was getting a holiday from school he replied casually, "*The teachers are all away being serviced.*"

Twins had just arrived in the class and the teacher said, "*Well, boys, how am I going to tell you apart?*"

"*That's easy,*" chirped up one of them, "*He's got a hamster, and I haven't!*"

The teacher was giving one little lad a row for getting so wet at play time. *"I told you to stay away from the puddles,"* she said, taking him by the scruff of the neck.

"But, Miss, it was the puddle that jumped up on me from somebody else, as I walked past."

The infant teacher was taking her new class round the school to show them where everything was. When they came to the dining room, one little lad piped up, *"Teacher, is this where we get our bar lunch?"*

My big brother has gone off to a bearding
school.

The headmaster called briefly to speak to the infant teacher with her new class. As he was leaving, one little fellow tugged at the teacher and asked, *"Please, Miss, what's he for?"*

The headteacher was visiting the new intake for the first time and was walking round the room to see what they were doing. He approached a little boy in the Wendy House but when he spoke to him the wee lad turned and walked away with, *"My mum says that I've not to talk to strange men."*

When the minister was visiting a home one day, the young son of the family, who had just started school, came into the living room.
"What did you learn at school today?" asked the man.
"The teacher taught us about saying 'yes miss' and 'no sir' to grown-ups,"
"Oh, you did, did you?"
"Ay!" was the quick reply.

There should be more parental involvement in class teaching.

Writing Wrongs

He was standing on the waters edge,
striped to the waist.

Write a sentence using the word *straightforward*.
My nose goes straightforward on my face.

He had a wide sombrero neatly erected on his head.

Her beautiful hare fell on to her bear shoulders.

It was my turn to be severed in the meat queue.

The woman always had plenty of money but it was clear that she was living off her immoral earings.

A white elephant is another name for a coward.

The Poll Tax will take the place of rats in every house.

A backbiter is another name for a flea.

Sailors in the navy can be noticed because they wear feeders on the back of their necks.

I was so excited that I ran home and toweled my father.

We climbed into the crib to see where many famous people were buried.

I enjoyed the film *Notre Damn.*

We were amazed to see Ivy climbing up the outside of the house and in the window.

One form of execution in the United States is the electric cushion.

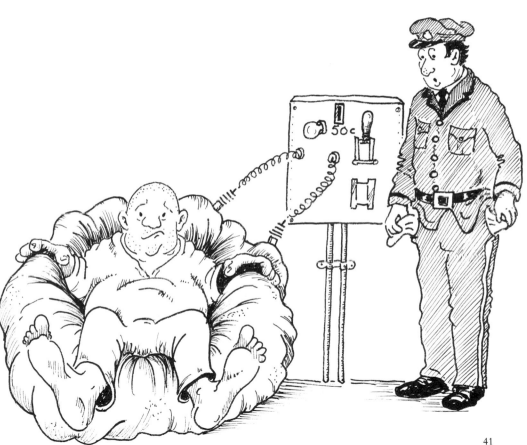

We were so tired that we just had a big cup of hot chocolate and fell in.

The prices in the local shop were realy exuberant.

We had peas, lame chops, cabbage and beans for dinner.

She lived in a large house on the superbs of the town.

42

No talking is aloud!

He was hot and thirsty so he sat down by a wayside inn and had a tanker of beer.

When an old man thinks of his young days he will think it ignorance to think silly things he knows better of now.

We had to wear nothing else except our belt and our haversack.

In the distance we noticed a large field of fur trees.

The police took very large steps to trap the road hog.

He sacrificed his life many times for his country.

"Rat tat tat", went the front door bell.

The well know poem begins, "Season of mists and melon fruitfulness . . ."

After the butler took in the old bags he introduced us to the rest of the family.

47

In olden days bores were hunted by dogs.

As we had plenty more time and it was a nice evening we decided to pull father out to see.

Dog Rose and Horse Radish are plants called after animals. Can you think of any more?
Collie Flower.

The subject I lick best is speling.

A half hysterical woman told the fireman that her old father was upstairs in bed with the flue.

There were over a hundred gusts at the party.

The Greek gods thought they were immoral so they had the time of their lives.

She laughed behind her breath.

She now lies in peas in a beautiful churchyard.

Complete these proverbs:

Its an ill wind . . . that blows from the
north.

that does everybody
good.

All's well . . . that eats beef.

that is not bad.

Two blacks . . . don't make a piece.

sing as nice as swallows.

Every cloud . . . has rain in it.

passes over in summer.

A stitch in time . . . stops you running.

saves you mine.

A rolling stone . . . stops eventually.

gathers the grass.

**There is a lot of punctuation in the
story. It helps the rabbit to express its
feelings to the horse.**

Record players used to be called grammar phones.

The teacher told us to sit on pears on the desks.

After a cordial farewell they climbed down the stars.

People who eat vegetables are called vergens.

There are few pursuits that a man can rise higher in than mountaineering.

The baby lamps sat all over the field at night.

Without cows we would have to go around in bear feet.

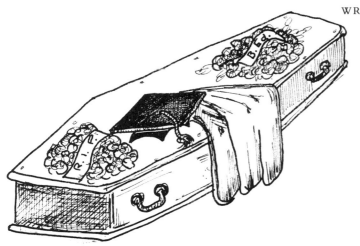

A post graduate is another name for a
dead teacher.

The antique dealer gave us a running
commentary on the table.

Because some of the old people in the home cannot climb the stairs they have built special wings for them.

I much prefer consecrated juice to artyficial.

He was well known as a truss worthy man.

When it got off the ground it was more than an hour over dew.

When you sneeze you should use atishoo paper.

My father has taken out a life membership of the national truss.

Dew is a sort of spittle on the grass in the morning.

On Saturday we went to a jungle sale in the church hall.

A gargoyle is a liquid used for a throatwash.

It was a big old house with ivory growing up the outside of the walls.

He was a tall seafearing man who loved boats.

She was swept away by a huge currant.

I had to go and get a massage for my mother.

I fell and hit my head and it was a while before I came to my censors.

The flames were coming up from the celery below. They had already burned away the ground floor.

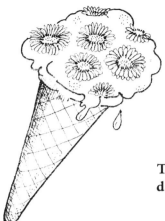

There is nothing better than real
daisy ice cream.

Every man on the sinking ship was
shaved including the ships cat.

I play the villain in the pantomime, but I didn't mind the hisses and the booze.

The tower of our school is one of the most outstanding obstacles in our town.

Etiquette is the noise you make when you sneeze.

Why does the author say that we should hold old people in respect?
Because they are the ones that generally have money.

There was not a sole on the boat until the kipper appeared from down below.

A beautiful paramour met his gaze as he reached the summit of the mountain.

We all went off in threes except for the two of us who went off in twos.

When the boy regained his conscience he landed up in hospital.

We went into a large hall in the school so that we could do Jim.

The dust can get into every crook and cranny.

He rushed over and gave the boy artificial perspiration.

In winter it is often very cold and sadly many old people die and go to heaven. Animals generally end up in a warmer place.

62

"*Now what would you find in air?*" asked the science teacher.
"*Please sir, Butlin's is in Ayr,*" replied one pupil without hesitation, "*I was there for my holidays last year.*"

"What part of the body is the trombone, Miss?"
"That's not a part of the body, Anne."
"It must be. The story says, 'After the concert it was dark and the man tripped and fell on his way home, breaking his trombone.'"

Sheep are sheared so they don't get hot in summer.

One of his plays was "A Sidecar Named Desire".

No pupil should leave school until he has mastered the basic three R's.

Please Miss, who cut the grass in the Garden of Eden after Adam was put out?

GARDENER WANTED APPLY WITHIN
EQUAL OPPORTUNITIES EMPLOYER

John Knox was a Protestant and the Church put him in prison for worshipping God.

Jesus taught a thick crowd a parable.

Day after day the Hebrew women had children in Egypt.

Hannah went to the temple and prayed for a baby. The very next day she had Samuel.

The pulpit is where the vicar perches every Sunday.

They washed their feet in Jesus time because they might have stood on something nasty on the way.

After doing a project on Holland the teacher was more than a little amused to read one child's R.E. notes: *Edam and Eve lived in the Garden of Eden.*

If Adam and Eve hadn't eaten those apples in the Garden of Eden, we probably wouldn't have to wear any clothes today.

A strict Scottish father reprimanded his children for playing at soldiers on the Sabbath.
"But, Dad, we're in the Salvation Army!"

People who are immortal can have the time of their lives.

The infants were rehearsing the Nativity Play for the school Christmas Concert. The little girl who was Mary, came up to the teacher and gave a big sigh. *"What's wrong dear?"* she asked.
"Oh, Mrs Thomson, it is awfully hard work being a virgin."

The story of the Early Church is found in the *Acts of the Impossibles.*

If a moslem is allowed more than one wife, how do they all get into a double bed?

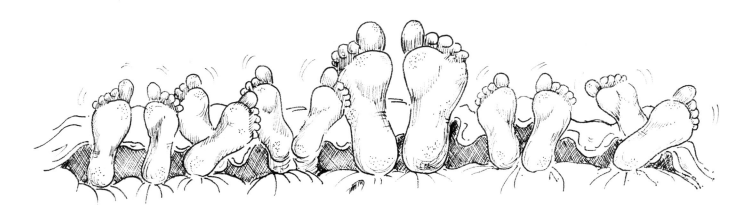

Jesus had lots of trouble with the Fairysees.

Robert Redford is Archbishop of Canterbury.

It was perhaps nearer to the point when one child wrote, *"Pontius Pilot washed his hands because he had blood all over them."*

I went to the school play last night. Every one knew their lines and no one had to be tempted.

What are priests called when they decide not to marry? *Bachelors of Divinity.*

We eat pancakes on stove Tuesday.

David fought the Philadelphian Giants with his sling.

A pupil who attended a non-denominational school learned that, if he had a note from his parents indicating that he was a Catholic, he need not come to classes until 9.30 a.m. once a week when the usual R.E. lesson was being given. After writing a note for himself he attended late each Thursday morning. The teacher's suspicions were aroused when he discovered that the fellow didn't attend classes organised for Catholic pupils either.
"You said that you were a Catholic, Danny," challenged the teacher.
"Yes, Sir, but that was only on Thursdays."

In India they throw people into the River Ganges so that they will go to heaven more quickly.

We were told that man's chief end was to glorify God and enjoy himself for ever.

The Jews do not worship in church they worship in a sin a gog.

My mum and dad go to the perish church on Sundays.

I suppose the expression *spoil the rod* must have meant that you had to give up fishing.

When was the Apostle Paul a baker?
When he went to Philippi (fill a pie).

Abraham nearly sacrificed his son Isaac because he had done a trick on Abraham and he didn't find it funny.

Who was very unhappy when the Prodigal Son returned to his father?
The fatted calf.

The people had lots of problems in these days with the Pharisees and the Seducers.

Paul was a tentmaker then he gave it up and became a Christian.

Confused by the Theory of Evolution one child asked, *"If God made Adam would that not mean that he was a monkey?"*

The rich man in the parable was called a fool because it would take him much more time to build a bigger barn and by that time all the crops would be dead.

**I wonder if Noah allowed a pair of
woodworms into the ark?**

A vicar wears a dress, wanders around with a big cross round his neck and is usually bald and smiling. He never goes out at night.

Children are turned into little cherrybins when they die.

On Christmas Day the minister was going round the pews talking to the children. One little girl said, "*If you hear a wee noise and smell a wee smell, Mr Jones, it's only me.*" She explained further, "*I got a watch and a wee bottle of perfume for my Christmas.*"

On hearing the story about the *Feeding of the Five Thousand*, when the disciples collected twelve baskets full of leftovers, one little girl piped up, "*My goodness, I hope Jesus put it in the freezer for another day!*"

A bishop wears a metre on his head.

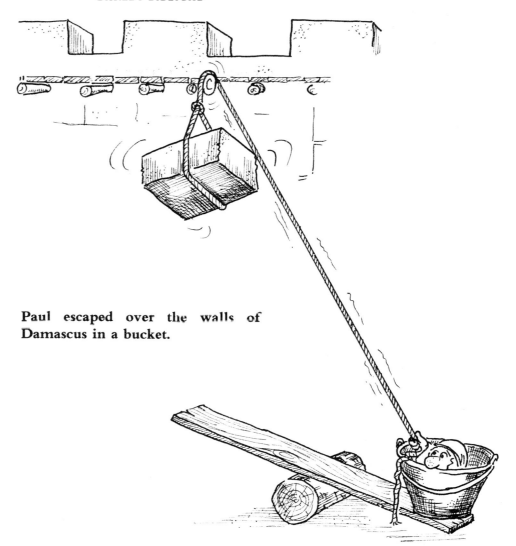

Paul escaped over the walls of Damascus in a bucket.

Mature teachers have a lot to offer the profession.

birds and bees

For Family Planning couples can use all sorts of different forms of contraptions.

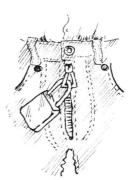

The relationship between them was mutual.

A kiss is better when the lips are coming together than after.

At school today our teacher told us all about starting a family (PTO) tree.

When I went to hospital I had to get my chest sexrayed by a special machine.

When one of her pupils announced that her mummy had just had a baby, the teacher remarked, "How nice, Susan! Is it a boy or a girl?"
"No, not yet, it's just a baby,"she replied.

Some infants were playing at "Mums and Dads" in the Wendy House. The teacher's ears pricked up when she heard the following:
"Push! Push! And watch out for the baby!"
When the teacher looked in to see what was being acted out, she was amused, and not a little relieved, to discover that a little girl was directing her "husband" to move the cooker for her.

The difference between a bee and a wasp is that a bee has a round end and a wasp has a sharp end.

"Mum, where were you and dad on the 15th September, 1975?" asked the ten-year-old, out of the blue, after sitting at the table for some time with a pencil and paper.

"How should I know?" asked mum, standing at the ironing table. *"Why are you asking anyway?"*

"Well we've been doing 'Living and Growing' at school and they explained how long it takes for a baby to grow. And I was working out my birthday and ..."

"Look, don't bother me just now, ask your father ..." came the evasive interruption.

A hereditary disease is one you can catch from your relatives. Like when my sister got chickenpox, I caught it too.

When visiting a farm with his class, the city child was fascinated to see milk being taken from a cow. Later on they were given milk to drink and scones with honey. *"Mmm, honey. Do you keep a bee as well?"* he asked intelligently.

Teachers nowadays are very aware that they must be careful when talking about *mummies and daddies* as there are so many one parent families. The fact was brought home to one teacher when observing children at play one day.

"If you don't behave yourself, I'll get a divorce and live with my other boyfriend!" announced one little girl to a little boy who wouldn't be bossed around by her.

87

Parents should be made more accountable
for their children's behaviour.

hardly historical

The Duke of Wellington got his name from the type of boots that he wore.

Stanley's first words were "Dr Lime-stone I presume?"

One of the greatest men to have lived in America was Martian Luther King.

In these days knights were shrivelless.

The man's family were condescendents from Bonnie Prince Charlie.

Marie Antoinette said, "*Let them have their cake and eat it.*"

The Battle of Haystrings was fought in 1066.

The King met the Barons at Runnymede for the Great Chatter.

Speaking about pollution on the River
Clyde, the teacher told the class that it was
said that King Robert the Bruce once
fished for salmon there.
*"Why would he not be able to catch salmon
today?"* asked the teacher. *"Because he's
dead!"* was the cheeky reply from one boy.

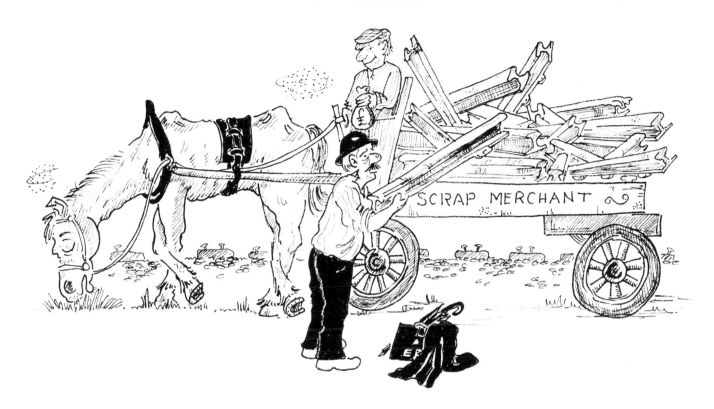

In the 60's Beeching was forced to lift
all the railway lines in order to make
ends meet.

Perhaps the Normans were more mechanised than hitherto realised for one pupil wrote: *They used a **battery** ram to attack castles and the Domesday Book was ordered by William I to work out the amount of **taxis** his subjects could afford.*

94

In Rome there has been very few
brakes in the chain of popes living in
the Vatican.

**Tollund Man was found when two
men were digging for Pete.**

Sir Walter Raleigh introduced tobacco and said, *"Today I have lit a fire in England that shall never be put out."*

Wellington was buried with full millinary honours.

The first wireless message came from a man that went through the air.

Shakespeare's father could not afford to give him a good education so he sent him to Oxford.

Cromwell died in constant fear of being murdered.

Galileo was the first man to make the earth go round the sun.

You can recognise Old Father Time because he carries a large cycle on his back.

The monasteries were dissolved because monks liked gamboling.

In Germany the Nasty Party took over and ran all over Europe.

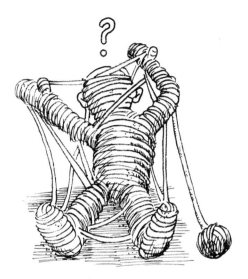

Mummies were Egyptians who buried themselves in bandages after they died so that they would live longer in the afterlife.

That type of farming suited middle aged people but they had to be prepared to work very hard.

Elizabeth Fry was a well known quacker.

Children were born every year in the 18th century.

Britain at that time had a very good navy and they were far better at fighting at sea than they were on land.

Samuel Pepys kept a dairy.

There was a drop of a hundred feet to the moat but it had no effect on the brave knight.

In the eighteenth century churches rented pews out for a prophet.

We do not know why Stonehenge was built but it certainly was built for some porpoise.

The armour was so heavy in those days that knights had to be lifted on to their houses with a crane.

January is named after the Roman goddess Janice.

During the war the propaganda machine told you what you should watch at the cinema.

During the Medieval Period people were sent out on pilgrimages so that they might repeat their sins.

Teachers should always set a good example to their pupils.

where in the world.?

In Norway there is a town called Hell, although it is really a cold country.

On holiday, we had sum difacutes with the langwig. But my dad new enouf french to get threw.

In Scotland the weather isn't very good but the climate doesn't happen every day.

Eskie Moes live in cold lands because it would be too far for them to travel to get heat.

When I go abrod I like to be in a place where there is see, sand and lots and lots of bitches.

The Legend is the part of the map which may not be true.

The Rhine flows horizontally through Switzerland and then it turns round and flows vertically through Germany.

If I had to live in a foreign country, I suppose I wouldn't mind East Anglia.

**Name five animals that inhabit the
Polar Regions?**
Three seals and two polar bears.

In cold weather the Eskimos turn their skins inside out to trap the heat.

Samson was caught by the Philippines.

Detergent is a special liquid for dissolving Greece.

Hans Christine Anderson was a very famous Danish writer.

My cousin came to visit us. He is an a stralyin.

In that country they make rubber by cutting the bark off a hyena tree.

To make the buildings in San Francisco safe from earthquakes they are built so that they don't quite touch the ground.

An Edinburgh teacher was talking to her class about the various Celtic languages and referred to the Welsh speakers.

"*Now, where in Scotland would you hear a language that you would not be able to understand?*" she asked pointing to the map. Without any hesitation, one pupil shouted out, "*Glasgow, Miss!*"

The first time I went on the boat to Ireland, I was very sick. My mother had a birth and she was alright.

If the wind is blowing from the North, which side of the school would you go to get shelter?
The inside, Sir.

"*Most people in our neighbourhood like to go on continental holidays,*" wrote a pupil. "*Not me! I can see all the sites I want to see here in Britain.*"

Parents don't appreciate teachers until it rains all day on a Saturday.

Sums + Segments

In our scicnce lab the biology teacher has put a brian into a big jar with water in it.

111

Every Spring our house is invaded by house martians.

Our teeth will go bad if you let the air get on to them.

How would you hatch eggs without the aid of a hen?
Use a duck.

Why is this year called a Leap Year?
Because it is the one year when a woman can 'leap' at a man.

"*Which is more, half an orange or eight sixteenth?*" was the trick question given to the class.
"*Half,*" answered one smart fellow. "*You would lose more juice cutting it into sixteen bits.*"

When air is inside a barometer a square inch weighs fifteen pounds.

Vitamin C helps to hold your hair in.

It is ill eagle to steal birds eggs from a nest.

My uncle in Caithness is a New Clear Santas.

Pure water must contain hydrogen because oxygen would just float away if it was not for the hydrogen.

The spinal chord keeps the back from doubling over and if the brain is injured it does the work of the brain.

You use a sandglass to boil eggs in.

The diafram is the lign through the middle of a circus.

When you look at a camel the first thing that strikes you is the huge hump. When you look closely the next thing that strikes you is the big hoofs.

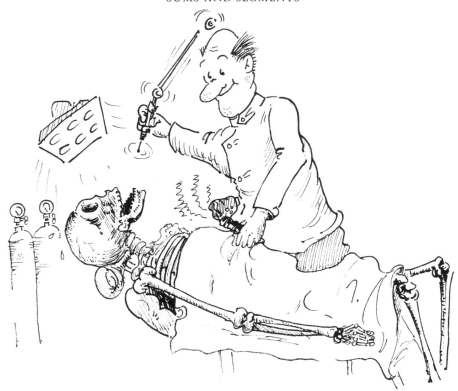

Nitrous Oxide is called Laughing Gas because when dentists used it the person on the chair became historical.

You must not let young children drink poison because they might not know what it is.

One seven-year-old was heard to remark just before a science lesson, "*Oh great, its science. I wonder if we'll have an experience?*"

The teacher filled the brunette from the science lab with alcohol.

"If I cut a piece of meat into sixteenths and then cut these pieces in three parts, what would I have?" asked the teacher. **"Mince, sir."**

A person who doesn't eat any fish, meat, eggs or plants and vegetables is called a vegan.

The Mail Order Protection Scheme means that you cannot try on underwear from a catalogue before you buy it.

I got my nose quarterised to stop it bleeding.

In the stomach the food is turned round and round and gets mixed up with ghastly juices.

The teacher was interested to know why one boy put off the light in the cupboard before he put the box of calculators on the shelf. *"I'm waiting for them to switch off in the dark in case the batteries run down,"* he replied, referring to the SOLAR machines.

If we are not careful decimals can burst our ear drums.

The Giant Banda lives in China which is black and white.

When they erupt lots of lager flows out of volcanoes.

**A lion is really just a tiger with black
and white dots.**

When buying a pair of cutting out shears it is important to consider what they sound like.

For school dinners we get low fat jelly for pudding.

There was no full moon for several months.

The camel is known as the sheep of the desert.

Any mother could cope with a class of five-year-olds.

Writes imaginatively: *particularly good at absence notes.*

Easily distracted: *never listens to a word I say.*

Very consistent work: *has failed every exam so far.*

Enjoys outdoor activities: *it would help if he came to school more often.*

He has a winning manner: *will be good with the pools.*

Satisfactory progress: *I've said that about everyone.*

He is good at sports: *certainly in for the high jump one of these days.*

Will go far: *the further away from here the better.*

Communicates fluently: *talks like a budgie.*

A solitary child: *has nits.*

Determined child: *lacks all scruples.*

Writing could be neater: *it's impossible to read it.*

Very bright, above average pupil: *thinks he knows more than the teachers.*

When a teacher introduced work cards to her class she was amused to learn from a parent one evening that her son had gone home and told her, *"We played card games for most of the afternoon."*

Every infant teacher keeps spare clothes in school for the little "accidents" which occur from time to time. One little girl wet herself and the teacher discreetly changed her and sent the soiled pants home in a carrier bag. Next day, travelling on the bus with her father, the little girl noticed her teacher in the seat in front of her and in a loud voice said, "Mrs MacFarlane, my daddy's got yer knickers in his pocket."

12

Peter, a bright five-year-old, was looking forward very much to starting school so his parents were a bit concerned when he came home after his first day, looking disappointed. *"That's it,"* he said to his mum and dad, *"I'm not going back there again!"* *"Why ever not?"* asked mum.

"Well, first of all, they never taught me to read and write. I got a silly wee book without any words to bring home and, worst of all, we got the story of the three little pigs, which I've heard hundreds of times from you already!"

All set to leave the house with her husband for a day in town one Saturday, the infant teacher turned to him and said, without thinking, *"Now, have you been to the toilet?"*

notice board

PINS MUST NOT BE REMOVED FROM THE BOARD

Found on the *floor* of a staff room:
Please replace drawing pins borrowed from this notice board.

School Canteen *Notice:* DESERT
CHOCOLATE MOUSE

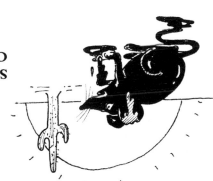

As the football pitch is waterlogged,
class 4a will do swimming instead.

NOTICEBOARD